J. B. ALBERT

24 Varied Scales and Exercises for Clarinet

ALLEGRO
EDITIONS

Published by Allegro Editions

Cover Image: *Circle of Fourths* by Marin Mersenne
Black and White Clarinet by Ron and Joe

Cover Design: Rachel Boothby Gualco

ISBN: 978-1-62654-0576

Printed and bound in the United States of America

24 VARIED SCALES AND EXERCISES FOR THE CLARINET
IN ALL THE MAJOR AND MINOR KEYS
by J. B. ALBERT.

he Student should play the following slowly at first, so as to familiarize himself with the difficulties of the fin-
ng; then increase the speed gradually.

Revised by
PAUL DE VILLE.

1. C MAJOR.

Nº 2. A MINOR.

23. F MAJOR.

Nº 4. D MINOR.

25. Bb MAJOR.

Nº 6. G MINOR.

Nº 7. Eb MAJOR.

№ 8. C MINOR.

side keys Fork keys

Nº 10. F MINOR.

Nº 12. Bb MINOR.

13. G♭ MAJOR.

Nº 14. E♭ MINOR.

15. B MAJOR. A# C# D# F# G#

Nº 16. G# MINOR.

No. 17. E MAJOR.

Nº 18. C♯ MINOR.

19. A MAJOR.

Nº 20. F♯ MINOR.

21. D MAJOR.

Nº 22. B MINOR.

23. G MAJOR.

№ 24. E MINOR.

9 781626 540577